GRACIAS, FIDEL!

A young boy's journey
escaping Castro's Cuba
and realizing
the American Dream

GRACIAS, FIDEL!

A young boy's journey
escaping Castro's Cuba
and realizing
the American Dream

NELSON A. DIAZ

Printed in the United States of America
Published in Hellertown, PA
Cover and interior design by Christina Gaugler
Library of Congress Control Number 2023904928
ISBN 978-1-958711-42-2

For more information or to place bulk orders, contact the author or the publisher at
Jennifer@BrightCommunications.net.

BrightCommunications.net

In memory of my father and mother,
Nelson Victor Diaz and Lucia Leonor Lacorra:
Their unconditional love for me was
their most valuable legacy.

PREFACE

You might find the title of this book intriguing, although I suspect that some Cubans who escaped Castro's regime may find the title insulting. *Gracias, Fidel* is not a political statement. I wrote it to share my life story and explain how I left my country and came to live in the United States. I believe my story can help inspire people—especially young people—who must leave their homes in search of a better life.

I know first-hand how difficult it is to leave a homeland. Suddenly having to flee and lose everything you've worked so hard to establish, as so many Cubans did, is agonizing, and starting from scratch later in life in a foreign country is challenging. It's easy to see how you might resent the people who forced you into such a painful upheaval.

I hope my book will inspire young people who find themselves in a similar situation to mine. All over the world, people face the same choices my family did to have a better future. Perhaps my book will offer a little hope to those who arrive here after escaping the tyranny and difficulties of their homelands.

I am grateful that my family made the painful decision to leave Cuba. Their courageous sacrifices gave me the opportunity to achieve a life for which I'm very thankful. That's why I chose the title of my book. Without the events that transformed Cuba, I would certainly not be here today to chronicle how I was able to realize the American Dream.

With my parents, Nelson and Lucia

My parents wedding in 1954

CUBA

CHAPTER ONE

HUMBLE BEGINNINGS

I'm 13, a strong, skinny, long-limbed boy. As my
mother, father, and great aunt Tati watch from an
open terrace atop the Havana Airport, I walk alone to
the Iberia Airlines jumbo jet idling on the tarmac. I
had never been to an airport before, and now my
family is waving me off as I leave my home for a boy's
camp across the ocean in Spain. It is February 1970.

I'm carrying the Bible that my father had given me
years earlier, in which he'd inscribed my name in his
beautiful handwriting. He gave me strict instructions
not to turn around and look back at my family. I had
never seen the inside of a plane, much less flown in
one. But here I am, about to soar into the sky and jet
nearly 5,000 miles to Madrid.

My journey to Spain began when my parents
started making careful, complicated plans for me to

escape my fate: I was to become a teenaged soldier in Castro's army. At that time in the 1960s, all Cuban boys were drafted in their 15th year to serve in the Cuban Revolutionary Army until the age of 27. Soldiers were not permitted to leave the country during their service.

My parents had a brighter future in mind for me, and it included finishing high school, attending college, and having the freedom to pursue my goals, wherever they might take me. Now, the only path to that future was for me to leave our family's home for a far-off foreign land.

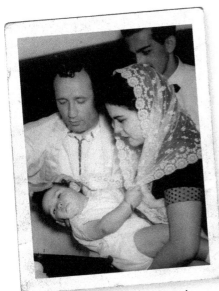

With my godparents, Aunt Rafaela and Uncle Rinaldo, during my baptism

My mother and father had always focused on improving my—and our family's— destiny. From my earliest childhood memories, my mother, Lucia Leonor Lacorra, told me that education was the key to getting ahead and to succeeding in life. Unlike many Cuban women

of her time, she'd managed to finish high school, and
she instilled in me her love of learning. I still remember
her drilling multiplication tables into my head and
going over my school homework every night.

My father, Nelson Victor Diaz, was a self-made man.
Not that he was rich—far from it. But thanks to his
resourcefulness and resilience, we were a comfortable,
lower middle-class family. By day, he was an *anotador*,
tracking the freight carried on ships. Cárdenas, my
hometown of about
80,000 people, was a

port city that attracted ships from all over the world, so there were plenty of vessels whose freight needed tracking.

After hours, my father had a small carpentry shop where he made furniture. Every stick of furniture in my home today was made by his hands.

El Espigón, Port of Cárdenas

I consider my father a true Renaissance man—he could do anything. He shared his knowledge with me—from carpentry and woodworking to killing and butchering animals for eating. He taught me how to fish and clean my catch, how to shine my shoes, and how to do the many chores it took to keep a small Cuban household running. For him, there was no sexist division of labor, as there was in many households. Over the years, he also taught me how to cook and iron.

How did my father learn all these survival techniques? I couldn't tell you. I suppose my father's talents came naturally to him. It's unlikely that he inherited any of those useful traits from his own father, who was a stern, nearly fearsome man who worked in the sugar cane industry.

My father was his father's opposite. Hand-in-hand, he'd take me to the ships he worked on, which was a huge treat for a little boy. I'd meet sailors from around the world, hear different languages, and get tours of their vessels. Those visits opened my eyes to the reality that many worlds existed outside of my own. My father brought me to his carpentry shop, too, where I learned how to hammer a nail, sand wood, and sweep the sawdust off the floor. I loved those days. I'd beg him to take me along and was teary-eyed when I couldn't go.

Until I was about four, we lived with my mother's parents in the center of Cárdenas. We lived happily together in a big, old-fashioned, colonial-style house. Our family was very close.

My mother's parents had divorced and remarried, and I was close to all of them—including my step-grandparents. In my mind, I had three sets of grandparents, all of whom were caring and kind to me. I spent a lot of time with my maternal grand-mother and her husband; he was another grandfather to me, and a very loving person. I used to spend weeks with them when I was little.

I called my *abuela* Tití. My step-grandfather's name was Julio and he drove a huge Indian motorcycle. That motorcycle (it would be quite the classic today) had a huge seat and was their main form of transportation.

My great-aunt Tati and me

When I used to ride with them, they'd put me in the middle between them. On longer rides, sometimes I would sleep in that cozy space. Because I could come and go at will between my parents and all my grandparents, I became a very independent kid, which served me well later in my youth.

During the summers, I also spent a month with my Aunt Rafaela, her husband, and my cousins on Cuba's beautiful Varadero Beach while my parents stayed home with my younger brother, Miguel, and my sister, Belinda. I also spent part of the summer in the relaxing fishing village of Playa Larga with my father's mother, Hortensia, and my cousins on my father's side.

My younger brother, Miguel, my sister, Belinda, and me

My Independent Boyhood

I certainly had been given the gift of independence. I'm pretty sure that today's notion of "helicopter parents," who manage every little detail of their children's existence, would have shocked, if not even angered, my mother and father. They were there to teach me important life lessons about how to take care of myself—and then they'd step back and let me learn, even if that meant watching me make mistakes. I think these lessons prepared me for what was to come because I was confident that I had the tools to handle pretty much any situation that came along. Little did I know at the time that just a few years later, these skills would end up practically saving my life.

Come the Revolution

I was born three years before the Cuban Revolution of 1959. Before the revolution, during the tyrannical seven-year rule of dictator Fulgencio Batista, my parents saw first-hand how badly poor people fared. Then along came the attractive firebrand revolutionary, Fidel Castro, with his bold promises to create a new Cuba. Fidel's Cuba would have democracy, free healthcare, and equality for all. Once again, Cubans would be able to own their own land and businesses. Castro even promised the entire world that his Cuba would be free of communism and the Soviet Union.

His declarations gave people like my parents reason to hope, and like many Cubans at that time they became early supporters of Castro and his revolution.

And hopeful things did come to pass. For example, we were able to move from the house we shared with my grandparents into a home of our own. At the beginning of the revolution, housing projects popped up all over Cuba. We secured a house in one of the developments, a cinderblock ranch that was ideal for me, my parents, and my younger brother and sister.

It had two bedrooms, a bathroom, a

Celebrating my birthday with my family and friends in our new home

living room, and a dining room, and we furnished it with pieces handmade by my father. Our new house was at the outskirts of Cárdenas, and my grandparents were now a few miles away. So, after school, I'd strap on my roller skates and skate over to visit them and play with my cousins.

It wasn't long before my parents recognized that Castro was not a man of the people—he was nothing but a cruel fraud. Despite Castro's promises to shun communist interference, in reality he had within months embraced the Soviet Union as a full partner and created a Cuban government based on the Communist model. He nationalized Cuban farms and businesses. He bent the education system to his will. He punished his political enemies (my father would become one of them) and arrested thousands—and worse.

Communism Comes to School

In the sixth grade, teachers had recognized me as the best male student academically in the entire city of Cárdenas. It was a very big deal—along with the best female student, I rode on a float in a parade through the city streets. Each year, the parade planners selected a different character for the winners to dress as

In the sixth grade, I was honored as the best male student in town

and this year, I was El Zorro, and my co-winner was costumed as his female partner.

From that moment of triumph, my schooling began to change. I didn't realize it then, but I was about to experience scholastic upheaval. Among Castro's influences on education, young students were now called "Pioneers." Though our math and science classes went on as before, in history classes the indoctrination into Communist principles began. Although my parents passed their convictions about freedom onto me and immunized me against becoming brainwashed, I still had to cope with the changes to the curriculum.

After Castro's takeover, he established the Cuban Revolutionary Armed Forces, and later, the Obligatory Military Service (SMO) system was created. This meant that boys had to join the army on January 1 of their 16th year, serve in active duty for three years, and then were committed to the army reserves until the age of 50.

My father wanted me to be free to attend college, and he wanted me to thrive based on my own abilities. He did not want me to enter Castro's army because he knew it meant spending the next decade or more of my life in captivity. Most of all, he didn't want to see me or my siblings succeed by losing our ideals and adapting to a communist lifestyle.

Besides advising the government that he was planning to leave the country; my father later sought a visa for me to leave to avoid the army. He soon learned how Castro treated those who didn't go along with the new regime. My father was fired from his job as an *anotador*—and the government even seized his little carpentry shop. I remember him telling me what he told the government officials who came to shutter his shop. "You can take my shop and my tools, but you can't take away what I know and what I can do with my hands."

The authorities sent him to a new job. He was to work in the tropical Cuban fields as a sugar cane cutter. It was back-breaking work, though I never heard him complain. We were only allowed to see him every 45 days when I'd go with my mother to bring him clothes and food. In all but name, my father had become a political prisoner, serving time at hard labor for the crime of wanting to be free.

And there were other terrible changes, too. For all sixth graders, the Revolution meant the end of those carefree, beachside summer vacations. Now, under Castro, we worked in the fields for a month each summer. The government owned all the farms now, and they needed workers. My job, under the merciless summer sun, was to pull weeds from endless rows of potato vines. In a brazen public relations attempt to put a positive spin on these child labor camps, the government called them "*escuelas al campo,*" meaning "schools in the countryside."

Looking back, I don't remember a school, I remember a prison. Dormitories were laid out military-style in tents with iron cots. We had common bathrooms with latrines dug into the earth—the flies and stench were overwhelming. The food came mostly from the Soviet Union—powdered milk, canned meat, bug-filled bread. The best part of any meal was Cuban style rice and beans.

The next summer, we were sent out to work for 45 days in the fields, and I graduated to hacking up yams so that they could be planted. I was given a rusty knife to do the job, and I remember cutting myself badly. I still have the scar.

Freedom: Leaving Cuba on a Jumbo Jet

As I said, my father's troubles began the day he advised the government that he wanted to leave Cuba. He lost his job, his carpentry shop, and his freedom—but he didn't lose his place in the lottery waiting to leave Cuba. Just several thousand visas were granted a year on a lottery basis for the Freedom Flights to Miami. You never knew when— or if—your turn to leave would come.

Because I was the oldest son, my father's priority was on getting me out of Cuba so that I could avoid being drafted. If that happened, I'd be stuck in Cuba for at least 10 years. After I

This photo was taken of my brother, my sister, and me the same day as my passport photo

got out, the rest of the family could wait and follow me when their turn came. We all waited breathlessly for my visa to arrive.

My father had discovered a program run by the Catholic Church in Spain. We had relatives who'd already left Cuba for America, and my father told them about the draft and the struggles we faced under Castro's regime. I believe it was my Aunt Belinda, then living in Indianapolis, who told my father about Father Camiñas—he's a mythic legend now—and his program to get boys out of Cuba to his camp in Spain. From there, the boys could get visas that allowed them to travel to the United States. A plan was born.

My aunt and other family living in America helped my parents get me a plane ticket to Madrid, the closest city to Father Camiñas's camp.

I was in my second year of "*escuela al campo*" in the seventh grade. I remember my mother and a neighbor named Mario—he was our neighborhood block's president and the only one with a government jeep—came to the camp to pick me up. It was dinnertime, and I was in the common dining area when I saw my mother entering with one of the teachers. She couldn't hide her joy, and she told me that we had received approval and the all-important visa for me to leave Cuba. I remember that many of the other kids congratulated me—and then asked me if they could keep some of my stuff, especially the food (pizza and dulce de leche) that my mother and Aunt Tati brought me on weekends. I also gave away my bedding and the mattress I got when I arrived at the camp.

Off to Havana

I remember my excitement and anticipation for this new twist in my life. It electrified me. I don't remember feeling scared at all—just the thrill most 13-year-olds experience when embarking on an amazing adventure. My mother and my Aunt Tati were crying the entire time, and I remember saying, "You don't have to cry. We'll be fine. I'm fine. You don't have to worry about me."

Now, as a parent myself, I realize that they feared the very real possibility of maybe not ever seeing me again—a prospect that never crossed my 13-year-old mind. Now that I'm a father, I also realize how protective one is of their kids when they're that young. As I think back, I understand my parents' fear for me, and I can see why they seemed so heartbroken.

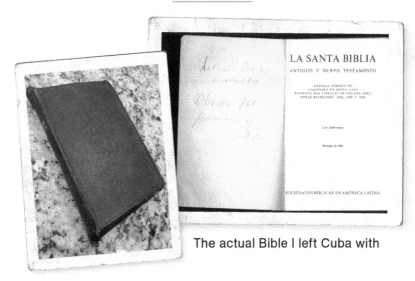

The actual Bible I left Cuba with

We arrived at Havana's José Martí Airport, and when it came time for me to board the plane, the airport people took us to this special room. They call it *La Pezera*—the Spanish word for "fishbowl." It was an all-glass room where you waited for your turn to board the planes idling on the tarmac below. It was time for me to say goodbye to my family.

My father's advice was stern as I held the leather-bound Bible he had given me several years before. First, he told me not to argue with any of the officials or airline personnel. And because we knew the Communists didn't respect religion, he told me to immediately surrender the Bible without argument if anyone asked me to. Finally, he said, no matter what, I wasn't to look back at them as I walked onto the plane. I wasn't to turn around or wave goodbye. My father warned me that I wouldn't actually be free of Cuban rule until I reached the plane, which officially was Spanish territory—so I'd better not call attention to myself by showing emotion.

I walked onto the tarmac toward the plane, clutching the Bible tightly in my hand, fearful of being stopped at any moment by the scary-looking men in uniform. When I was close enough to hop on the plane by outrunning anyone who tried to stop me, I turned my head to look back at my family.

I found their tear-stained faces quickly among the crowds on the airport terrace. Once I had them in my sights, I smiled as broadly as I could, waved with one hand, and with my other hand, I held the Bible high over my head. That was how I said goodbye to my family and assured them that I was going to be all right.

SAN LORENZO DE EL ESCORIAL

CHAPTER 2

ALL ABOARD: MY JUMBO JET TO FREEDOM

As I boarded the Iberia Airlines jumbo jet, the steward-esses (as flight attendants were then called) greeted me warmly. I'd never seen such beautiful women. To me, they were compassionate goddesses in uniform. They treated us as if we were precious cargo. I say "us" because it turned out that I was one of seven little Cuban boys flying alone to Madrid. It must have been clear to the crew that none of us had ever been away from our mamas and papas before. One boy, the smallest of us, cried during the entire seven-hour flight, despite our best efforts to comfort him.

I was in awe as one of the stewardesses directed me

to my seat, where, like any kid, I immediately started playing with the air-conditioning knob, the lights, and the window shade. The stewardesses handed us blankets, pillows, and slipper socks. I was dumbstruck to experience such over-the-top kindness and generosity.

Unlike my inconsolable little flight companion, I was flying high both literally and spiritually on this adventure. I felt like an astronaut, a pilot, a pioneer. I was setting a course for my new life, a life that would be far from the Cuban fields and forced toiling under a broiling sun. Though I had no idea what lay before me, I had only excitement for the future—no fear whatsoever.

We landed in Madrid early on a chilly February morning, and I remember seeing the foggy mist outside the airplane's windows. I felt as if I'd fallen under a magical spell. Madrid-Barajas International Airport was huge, impressive, and very, very busy. I'd never seen anything like it.

A representative from the Catholic church met us at our gate. He explained that we would be in his care, and we called him *"El Mando,"* meaning authority. He and his wife lived in the church-sponsored camp for Cuban boys escaping the military, and they were responsible for caring for me and the other boys.

Freedom and Fighting in Spain

As I walked through the airport, I suddenly realized that I wasn't in Cuba anymore. I was in Spain, where I could buy and eat anything I wanted—no more buggy bread! When the kindly *El Mando* asked if we wanted anything, I asked for a Coca-Cola and chewing gum. He put some coins into a vending machine and handed me those magical treats.

Then, like a flock of ducklings, we seven boys followed *El Mando* into Madrid's subway—another dazzling experience. We were on our way to meet Father Antonio Camiñas, the priest who was responsible for the Cuban boys' rescue program. We were to join him at his cathedral in Madrid.

When we arrived, the path to Father Camiñas's office took us through the dim, ancient-looking grandeur of the cathedral. As *El Mando* led us through the maze inside of the church, with its endlessly high ceilings, grim-faced statues, bloody crucifixes, stained glass windows, and elaborate carvings, I prickled with terror. Could this be my new home? The thought of living in such a dark, morbid place terrified me. What had I gotten myself into, I wondered. Never being the bashful sort, I blurted out the question.

To my relief, *El Mando* smiled and replied that we

had just stopped at the cathedral to pay our respects to Father Camiñas and that our final destination would be the camp called Santa Maria del Buen Aire Youth Hostel, located in the town of San Lorenzo de El Escorial. The town, located northwest of Madrid, contains the Royal Monastery of San Lorenzo de El Escorial built by Spain's King Phillip II in the 16th century. Today, it is a tourist mecca.

We met Father Camiñas in his office, where he greeted us warmly and offered us some olives. Looking back, I remember how good the olives tasted. I'd never before eaten or even seen olives, which don't grow in Cuba, and after Castro's revolution I imagine they'd be a luxury known only to government officials.

After our visit, *El Mando* led us into the subway, which we took to Atocha Railway Station, a huge, grand, elegant train station—think Grand Central Station in New York City. From there we had about an hour's train ride to *El Escorial*, which we finally reached around dinnertime.

Santa Maria del Buen Aire camp

So, there we were—seven completely exhausted, starving young boys. We'd barely slept on the plane, and we hadn't eaten all day—unless you count the olive offering from Father Camiñas.

At the camp, we were led into a dining hall where tables were set up cafeteria style. Each of us was assigned to a different table, and each table had a head boy who was in charge of serving the food from the large bowls coming out of the kitchen.

In an instant, the magic of this wonderful new experience evaporated, and things turned ugly fast. The head boy at my table said, "The new ones are not eating tonight," and they pulled our plates away from us. This action by the head boy was called "the stabbing," and it was how the boys greeted most of the new arrivals. All of us new boys had to watch hungrily while the others wolfed down their food. And then our situation got even worse. As we left the dining hall, the "old" boys began beating up on the new boys. They were taunting us, pushing us, hitting us—it was a terrible sort of hazing.

I yelled out a curse about their mothers—a vulgar insult—and that enraged the old group and singled me out as the new group's troublemaker. We were about to cross a little bridge over a creek to get to our quarters, and I could see the boys—around 40 of them—lined up on either side. We had to pass between two lines of them, and they beat me as I passed through. When I finally fell into my cot, I stuffed my blanket in my mouth. I refused to let them hear me cry.

Life at El Escorial

The hazing and the terrible treatment lasted about a week. We were constantly bullied—until the next group of new boys arrived from Cuba. I'm a little ashamed to say how relieved I was to now become one of the "old" boys. I joined in with the gang as they hazed and beat up the new arrivals. I was terrified not to and felt the pressure to fit in, so I participated.

Though *El Escorial* was certainly a better situation than the one I'd experienced at "escuela al campo" in Cuba those two summers, it was still pretty rugged. The dormitories were on the other side of the creek from the dining hall. They were long one-story struc-tures, separated into small rooms that held two bunkbeds. Each building had two wings with a center social area that had a TV, as well as lavatories with showers. There was no hot water, though, so the showers were freezing. I would do jumping jacks before hopping in, just to get a little warmed up. The

The camp

camp was used by the Spanish youth during the summer, and it was not equipped for the cold of winter.

It surprises me now to realize how little supervision we had at the camp. Although *El Mando* and his wife were on hand to provide some oversight, they stayed indoors much of the time, so we were pretty much left to our own devices. We didn't take classes or have any schoolwork to do.

We didn't see much of Father Camiñas either. I remember he visited the camp just once while I was there. I also remember that a countess once visited us. She apparently provided financial support for the program, and she arrived in a shiny stretch limousine. It was the first time I'd ever seen a car that big. I remember that she stepped out of her car and hugged us all.

Perhaps because there was so little supervision, the boys staged lots of fighting games, including a terrifying one called *pilitas*. In this "game," the head boy and leader of the group chose a boy to lie down on the ground, then the rest of us would pile on top of him. It was pretty scary if you were one of the boys on the bottom because it would be so hard to breathe. We also had bare knuckle fights, which would be stopped when one of the fighters started to bleed.

Despite these "games," life in *El Escorial* was mostly dull and boring. I was homesick for my family back in Cuba. Sometimes on the weekends, the other boys and I would head to the café in the center of town to play pool and pinball. The song *"Cuando Salí de Cuba,"* which I had never heard before, often played on the jukebox. The song starts with the line, "When I left Cuba, I left my life, I left my love." I still get emotional thinking about it.

I spent a lot of time writing to my parents and to my family in Cuba. I would tape chewing gum inside the letters to send to my brother, sister, and cousins.

Still, I occasionally managed to create my own excitement. Using

Enjoying Spain with my friends Magdaleny and Geraldo

the little bit of cash my family sent me, every now and then I'd travel to Madrid by train and subway to visit a family friend of ours who had lived next to my grandfather in Cárdenas. They'd take me to the parks and to the zoo with their children Magdaleny and Geraldo.

My stay in Spain taught me how to be independent, how to rely on myself. You could say that I skipped being a teenager. I went directly from childhood to adulthood, and I missed having that carefree life most teenagers know.

Leaving for America

My stay at *El Escorial* lasted about four months, from February of 1970 until that June. I was one of the lucky ones because my father's older sister, my Aunt Belinda, sponsored me for a visa to leave Spain for America. The children who had no sponsors ended up spending a much longer stretch in the camp.

So, now I embarked on another adventure. It began the day that *El Mando* came to tell me that my paperwork was in order, and I would soon depart for the United States. In preparation for leaving, he took me to Madrid's old, famous department store, *El Corte Inglés*, comparable to a Macy's. The store had a

Getting ready to leave Spain for the United States

tradition of supplying each camp boy with a pair of shoes, a shirt, pants, tie, and a sports jacket before they left Spain for the US. It's possible that either the store itself or the countess paid for each child's new suit. I remember getting all dressed up in my "traveling clothes" and standing proudly as the store's photographer took my portrait.

I was thrilled that I was finally going to reunite with my family, especially my Aunt Belinda and Uncle Amado. I couldn't wait to experience life in the US, especially because I remembered talking with my parents back in Cuba about how grand, open, and free it was there.

I finally left Madrid in June of 1970—my four-month stay seemed like an entire lifetime to me. I wore my stylish new outfit for my plane trip, and a name tag hung around my neck. I was only 13 and making my second solo transoceanic voyage. I was happy to discover that these stewardesses spoke Spanish, which made the flight feel familiar and pleasant. Still, it felt like a very long trip.

When I arrived at the Pan Am terminal at JFK, I was met by a woman who took me to the TWA terminal for my connecting flight to Indianapolis. Unfortunately, the crew aboard this flight didn't speak Spanish, and I was both panicked and confused when the plane made a stop somewhere in Ohio that I had not expected.

Should I stay on board? Should I get off? The stewardess couldn't understand my questions, and I worried that I was going to make a mistake. The stewardess took me off the plane and went with me to the service counter off the jetway to check my documents with the service personnel. After that, she took me back to my seat on the plane. I can still remember the sigh of relief that escaped me when I was back on the plane as it took off for Indianapolis.

INDIANAPOLIS,
INDIANA

CHAPTER 3

MEETING MY AMERICAN FAMILY

My Aunt Belinda and Uncle Amado picked me up at the Indianapolis International Airport. Even though I hadn't seen them for years, I recognized them immediately. My parents kept their pictures in our house in Cuba, so I certainly knew what they looked like— and when I saw my aunt face-to-face, I knew she was family. I had brought gifts for them: for my aunt, a little pair of Flamenco dancers, and for my uncle, a bull and matador—typical touristy trinkets that I'd bought at an airport gift shop. Despite how cheap looking they must have been, they loved their gifts and told me how much they appreciated them.

It was now early June of 1970. My aunt and uncle lived in a two-bedroom ranch house in the neighborhood of Lawrence, a comfortable, middle-class suburb of Indianapolis. Aunt Belinda was a middle school Spanish teacher, and Uncle Amado was an RCA employee. They both worked during the day. The night before I was to spend my first day alone in the house, my aunt showed me where everything was in the kitchen and taught me how to make a ham and cheese sandwich.

Their son and only child, my cousin, also named Amado, was away serving in the Air Force. I was given his bedroom, which was loaded with luxuries I had never dreamed of having. A TV and a record player of my own—imagine! I felt like I was in heaven.

I worked hard to make myself useful to my aunt and uncle. They owned two cars, both Chevrolets—an Impala and a Corvair. I decided it would be my job to scrub them inside and out every week. When Uncle Amado saw my interest in their

My Aunt Belinda and Uncle Amado

cars, he taught me how to check the oil and fluids. He also taught me how to start them up and move them so that they were closer to the water hoses. I was so happy to earn his trust, and I loved starting the engines in the morning for them. These skills would come in handy in a few months when I was able to leverage my basic automobile knowledge into a paying job.

Uncle Amado also taught me how to mow the grass. When he saw how much I enjoyed doing it, he helped me set up my own lawn mowing business. He let me use his mower and encouraged me as I went from house to house seeking work from the neighbors. It was the first time I was making my own money, and it sent my self-confidence into the stratosphere. Now I could buy my own clothing and other necessities. Uncle Amado was the one who fueled my desire to make my own money—and later to become an entrepreneur.

Aunt Belinda and Uncle Amado became my second parents. They loved me and treated me like their own son. Because their son was away in the Air Force, they probably were happy to have a young boy around who they could parent in his place. I loved them both dearly and miss them to this day.

Even though I was mature and responsible for my age, there were many skills I needed to acquire. My aunt, for example, taught me proper table manners: the correct posture for sitting at the dinner table, how to hold and use utensils, and how to converse in a quiet tone of voice. I remember my first trip to a big American store with my aunt and uncle. I was amazed at its size and variety of goods for sale. My aunt was shopping on one side of the store, and I was on the other. And in Spanish, I screamed out, "Tía! Tía!! Look at this!" She hurried over to me, glanced at the object of my fascination, and then spoke very softly to me, also in Spanish, almost whispering: "My nephew, in this country, people talk quietly. They don't scream."

Her whispering to me made a point that has stayed with me to this day. In this country, people tend to be a bit more reserved. They don't speak loudly or scream out or even play music loudly in public, all of which were acceptable in the culture I came from. I needed to learn how to communicate a bit more calmly if I wanted to assimilate into my new country.

Clearly, all those noisy boys at my Spanish camp reinforced behaviors that now I would definitely need to forget.

I loved being part of the Cuban community of Indianapolis, which my aunt and uncle introduced me to. It was its own small world, and many of its members were related to each other. This was a warm and happy time for me—friends, family, and neighbors all treated me well. No one was a foreigner or a stranger. All the kids wanted to be my friend, and I felt as popular as a movie star.

On the weekends, we used to visit my uncle's family, where everyone was kind to me. I turned 14 that summer, and I remember they threw me a party, complete with presents. I felt like I was surrounded by love.

My Aunt Belinda and Uncle Amado in their home in Indianapolis

Starting School, Learning English

Because my aunt was a teacher, she was able to enroll me in summer school so that I could learn English. She drove me there an hour before school started, and she arranged to have a speech therapist work with me privately during that hour. Using flash cards, the therapist taught me correct pronunciation. Working intensely like this allowed me to pick up English pretty quickly, and soon I was using English words and speaking in short sentences.

I was too young to know about dating, but I hung out with a girl I liked a lot. I thought of her as my girlfriend, and mostly we just tried to communicate with each other. I used an English-Spanish dictionary to translate our chats—being motivated by puppy love certainly improved my English! I learned how to say, "I love you" very quickly. She invited me to her house to meet her family. Her mother offered me a slice of warm pumpkin pie. I'd never had a warm dessert before and thought it was pretty weird. I didn't like it, but I didn't let on. I ate it by alternating each piece with a drink of water.

I made steady progress with my language studies. I

felt like I had no other choice if I wanted to enjoy my new life. The only place I spoke Spanish now was at home with my aunt and uncle or with other members of my Cuban family.

In school, I was the only Spanish-speaking student and, as far as I remember, the only foreigner. So, I immersed myself in the English language and American culture and learned both as quickly as I could. Even though I couldn't fully communicate with my new friends, they accepted and embraced me. It seemed like everyone in school wanted to hang out with me. I was living a teenager's dream. My new friends' parents took me to parks and the community swimming pool. I remember how shockingly cold the water felt compared to the beautiful, warm Cuban beaches.

Once school began in September, I was enrolled in the eighth grade—even though I hadn't finished seventh grade back in Cuba. Though I was way behind in English, I was able to cope pretty well with my math and science classes. I found that I was able to understand the science terms, which come from Latin, so they were familiar to a Spanish speaker. I was proud of myself for being able to do so well in such a short time.

Although I was the only immigrant in my school and in the neighborhood, I never felt any prejudice from any of my new American friends. I felt completely embraced by them and their desire to help me. Although my grasp of English was far from perfect, I adapted very quickly to my new life. This lesson taught me that young immigrant children should be immersed into their new setting as quickly as possible.

Looking back, I think that when you find yourself in a "sink or swim" situation, you learn and do what you can to stay afloat very quickly in order to survive.

Bittersweet Joy

One day shortly after the new school term began, Aunt Belinda took me aside. She told me that my family had finally been awarded their visas, and they were about to make the short journey to Miami. True to the indifferent way in which the Cubans treated their citizens, my family only got a few days' notice before they had to pack up their allowed amount of clothing and leave the country without any possessions or money. In just a few weeks, I would fly down to Miami to join them. Little did I know how much my life was going to change—again.

MIAMI, FLORIDA

CHAPTER 4

LIFE IN MIAMI, MILLIONS OF MILES FROM INDIANAPOLIS

In October of 1970, the phone rang at Aunt Belinda's house. When my aunt put me on the call, I heard my mother's voice for the first time in months. She was calling from Miami! Finally, at long last, my parents and my little brother and sister had escaped Cuba and made it to America. My mother cried tears of joy when she heard my voice after our long separation.

My family was admitted to this country thanks to the sponsorship of my father's younger brother, Rinaldo. My uncle and father were close in Cárdenas, and my uncle, who had emigrated to Miami in the 60s, was already established there. Besides being a

My parents with my Uncle Rinaldo and his wife Oneida in Cuba around 1954.

butcher in a grocery store, he also ran a side business painting new construction projects. He needed help, so I think he convinced my father to stay in Miami even though my parents' original plan was to go on to Indianapolis.

Before my family left, things in Cuba had changed for them. The government pulled my father out of the sugar cane fields and stationed him in the city of Matanzas, about an hour away, where they assigned him to help rebuild the city's port. The officials must have realized that his finely honed carpentry skills were wasted in the fields cutting sugar cane. The need for trained carpenters, especially those with some knowledge of ships, was urgent because Castro was renovating the port of Matanzas so that Russian military ships could dock there.

My mother's family had to support her as she

waited for our family's visas to come through. She sold her jewelry and her few family heirlooms so that she could feed my little brother and sister while my father was away. Life under Castro continued to be cruel to my family—although my father was no longer slaving under the sun in the miserable sugar cane fields, he was still separated from his family, and their financial situation was desperate.

Crowding into Miami

My father traded our somewhat comfortable life for years of deprivation and sacrifice in the desperate hope that doing so would help him secure a better future for all of us. It took years, but eventually my family's visas came through and they were able to get four seats on one of the Freedom Flights leaving Cuba for Miami in the early fall of 1970.

Once my family's visas arrived, they boarded a flight to Miami. The city was a natural magnet for Cuban immigrants. Spanish was spoken, the weather felt like home, and shopkeepers sold products familiar to us.

When my parents, brother, and sister landed, the plan was for them to move into a small, two-bedroom apartment with my Aunt Hortensia, Uncle Wilfredo, and cousin Bibiana. It was a temporary step before they found their own apartment, but it was a difficult one. Seven people in that small apartment was a very tight squeeze.

Because there was no room there for me to join them, I couldn't move to Miami until my parents got their own place. Soon, they found a one-bedroom apartment in the same complex as my aunt and uncle, and I flew down to Miami to join them.

Now five of us jammed into a one-bedroom apartment. It was a drastic change for me. I went from having my own bedroom to sharing a single bed with my brother, Miguel, while my sister Belinda slept on the living room couch. Our apartment complex was a block away from the fire department and a railroad

The apartment building where I lived with my parents and siblings in Miami

crossing. It was also a mile or so from the Miami International Airport and directly in the flight path of one of their landing strips. It was a night and day difference from Aunt Belinda's quiet Indianapolis suburb.

I still remember the relentless noise. It was enough to drive anyone insane, especially a boy who had gotten used to living in a quiet, peaceful suburb. The apartment's windows rattled loudly every few minutes whenever jets landed or took off. The sounds of sirens and train whistles were constant. It felt like the whole apartment was permanently shaking.

I was happy to be with my parents and siblings again, but our apartment was a difficult place to live, and I missed my life and friends back in Indiana.

Our apartment complex was in a treacherous section in Miami northwest. Uncle Rinaldo, my father's younger brother, told my parents to enroll me in a school that served Miami's nicer southwest side where the most established Cubans lived, and where he lived with his family.

Soon after I enrolled and started classes at the "good" school, the authorities caught me and told me I was in the wrong district. That's when I found myself starting eighth grade for the third time that school year, this time in a school in the poorer neighborhood where we lived.

My new school was mostly attended by black and Cuban kids, and the relationship between the two groups was tense. I think that the tension was based on competition for jobs. Poor people in Miami feared that the large wave of new Cuban immigrants would take their jobs and other resources.

I learned that I had to align with one group or the other just to stay out of trouble. Naturally, I aligned with the Cuban and Hispanic kids. I remember that fights broke out nearly every day after school. Actually, the boxing skills I'd learned in Spain came in handy, as I'd learned how to protect myself as well as how to fight.

Looking back, all I really remember was the fighting. When it comes to my school days, I remember nothing. I guess that tells you what really impacts a teenage boy's mind. Though I didn't know it at the time, it turned out that I'd only be in Miami for a few months before our family moved to New Jersey. So, the most dramatic parts of my short Miami stay were what my brain retained—and that was the fighting, not the schoolwork.

The battles took the form of kids attacking each other mostly from a distance, throwing rocks and sticks. Rarely was there any boy-on-boy fighting. Luckily, no one had weapons—certainly no guns or knives. We were only 14, and in reality, we weren't all that tough, despite our tough-guy attitudes. I supposed we imagined ourselves to be little gangsters. Although I now realize this might not have been a life-threatening situation for me, like the bloody and sometimes fatal gang fights you see in the movies, it felt that scary to me at the time. It was a tough, traumatic way for a kid to live each day.

I found my new way of life shocking. I'd never been involved in racially motivated fights before. One thing about Cuba when I was growing up was how multicultural it was, with all the ethnic groups easily blending together socially and getting along with each other. In Cuba, I had friends of all colors whose ancestors came from all around the world. In Indianapolis, I'd made friends with everyone immediately, even though I spoke only a few words of English.

It was a different story in Miami. Each ethnic group kept to itself, and each group resented people from other backgrounds. All of this was bewildering to me. And if the constant racial tensions, the relentless noise, the terrible school, the crowded apartment, and the fighting weren't challenging enough, we also had to cope with being dirt poor.

Everything seemed harder for us in Miami. Take shopping, for instance—it was a terrible chore. I remember we used to walk for what seemed to be miles to buy food at one of the larger grocery stores because prices at our local market were sky high. We would all trek back to our apartment with plastic bags full of food. I remember my little sister, Belinda, and brother, Miguel, who were just six and eight at the time, helping carry the bags. The walk was long, and the Miami heat was intense.

We just barely scraped by on my father's paycheck. He made $70 a week, and he had to take several buses each day to his job in a furniture factory. My uncle's side painting business had collapsed, and my father was the only one working—those earnings just couldn't support us all.

Although our stay in Miami was short, I managed to find a job in a gas station after school. The skills I learned taking care of my uncle and aunt's car, and the desire to earn my own money from my lawn-cutting business in Indianapolis, came in handy. Besides helping my family with the little bit of money I made, I also managed to save enough to purchase a small battery-operated radio and cassette player.

In a cruel twist of fate, when my family finally

landed in Miami, they found that life there was every bit and difficult and challenging as Cuba had been. Freedom, they discovered, doesn't mean much if you can barely afford groceries, you're subject to ear-shattering sirens and air traffic 24/7, and your safety is in jeopardy.

Because of my father's difficulties in finding a better-paying job, due to the lack of transportation and the intense competition from new immigrants, my father started to explore other options. He called his cousin Antonio (everyone called him Coco), who lived in Vineland, New Jersey, to see if better opportunities existed there.

VINELAND,
NEW JERSEY

CHAPTER 5

MOVING NORTH SAVED OUR FAMILY

Even after we had begun settling into our new New Jersey life, my parents, especially my father, knew that they had made painful sacrifices to protect our family from the indignities that Castro had inflicted on Cubans. When my father took the gamble of sending me, his first-born son, off to Spain to escape the army and its decades-long service commitment, he lost his comfortable job. The government seized his little carpentry shop, and for all intents and purposes, he became a political prisoner sentenced to hard labor in the sugar cane fields.

So, a few months after my father called his cousin Coco about job prospects up north in Vineland, New Jersey, he made the decision to move us from Miami to Vineland. Vineland is a small city in southern New Jersey. It is approximately an hour southeast from Philadelphia.

Coco had settled with his family in Vineland some years before. He had done well for himself and was fairly well established. He told my father of the work opportunities available in the small city, that there would be work for him and my mother, and better educational opportunities for my siblings and me. Coco generously invited us to live with his family until my parents started to work and could rent their own place.

My father decided to move us north to find a better life. In February of 1971, my family made the north- ward move.

We moved in with Coco, his wife Elba, and their daughter, Elbi and son Tony. They had a two-bed- room house, and it was a tight squeeze—now, nine people crammed into a house barely big enough for

Coco and his wife, Elba

four. I'm sure this was a sacrifice for Coco's family, but they made us as comfortable as they could, and welcomed us graciously.

Almost as soon as we'd unpacked, my mother landed a job in a factory that made military clothing, and shortly after that, my father also got a job in the cleaning department for Venice Maid, a food factory. Two paychecks meant a much easier life for our family. In Vineland, life was finally looking up for the Diaz family.

In time, our situation became much more comfortable. At Venice Maid, my father's talents were recognized. He was promoted many times, eventually becoming a first-class cook, then finally taking charge as the lead mechanic with a much higher salary.

As my father progressed up the ladder at Venice Maid, he began to collect carpentry, plumbing, and electrical tools, and before long he had a side job as a handyman for various realtors and investors. He maintained those two jobs in Vineland until his death.

Living as a Cuban Again

In Vineland, things were also looking up for me. My two cousins, Elbi and Tony, were around my age, and they had also lived in Cárdenas, Cuba where we spent time together. We reacquainted immediately. Soon, I became part of their circle of friends, and fun trickled back into my life.

Within a few weeks, my father was able to sign a lease for our own one-bedroom apartment. It was in a converted single-family house in the center of town, and it had an unusual layout. The living room was on one side of the apartment, then there was a staircase to a third-floor apartment, and our kitchen, bathroom and bedroom were on the other side. I slept in the living room. To join the rest of the family, I had to unlock a door to get into their side of the apartment. But at least it was quiet. There were no jet planes or screaming sirens like in Miami. That's because, although Vineland is now New Jersey's third-largest city by size, it was quite rural at that time.

Then, in just a year or so after we'd moved in, we were able to move out of the odd-shaped rental to an apartment complex, and then buy a small house—and even a car. Thanks to my father's hard work, our family was prospering financially, and my mother was even able to become a full-time housewife again, and she took pride in caring for our family

We found ourselves living in a mostly Cuban

community. It was small—just 100 families or so—and most people came from my hometown of Cárdenas. We all knew each other or were related by blood somehow, so we formed an extremely supportive network. We helped each other with housing and jobs. My family reconnected with old friends they'd known in Cuba.

I certainly didn't miss Miami or its gang violence. In fact, there was no violence at all in the school in Vineland that I can recall. If anything, I might have felt a sense of segregation, not discrimination, because we were living almost as we had back home in Cuba, surrounded with people very much like us. Most of my new friends were Cuban, and we belonged to a Cuban club, *Liceo Cubano*, which had a youth group—of which my cousin Elbi was the president. Meetings were held at Coco's house, and that's where I formed some lifelong friendships.

For example, I met my best friend, Julio Mendez, who I consider a brother to this day. Funnily enough, though we attended the same middle school in Cuba, we never met there. But we became business partners and invested in real estate together decades later in America. I also met a lovely young woman with curly hair named Silvia, who would become central to my life.

I readjusted to my new life in Vineland quickly, and my new friends helped speed my transition. I found a job in a gas station owned by Juan Enrique, a legend among the Cuban community. There, many Cuban men would stop for coffee each morning to talk and joke. I learned other skills there, and soon was able to change the oil, fix brakes, do tune-ups, change and fix tires, and many other repairs. I eventually left Juan Enrique's gas station to work with his son Carlos when he opened his own gas station.

Learning to Overcome Challenges in School

Despite the good things that were happening for my family in Vineland, my school life was troubled. For the fourth time in less than a year, I'd enrolled in a new school in the eighth grade. Looking back, I realize that my experiences at the Spanish camp and in Miami had changed me from the gentle little boy I'd been into an angry teenager who always felt he had something to prove. I'd learned how to defend myself in the Spanish camp and on the streets of Miami, but I'd been so traumatized by the bullying and fighting that I swore I'd never be bullied again. I developed a tough guy attitude, and a "better to hit than be hit" mentality.

As I result, I got myself into a lot of fights. What's worse, that big chip on my shoulder stood in the way of my succeeding in school. Both my parents were frustrated to see me veer off the path they'd worked so hard to create for me.

Thinking back on this now, I wonder how a boy with such promise and potential—I had been lauded as Cuba's best sixth grade student—could become so difficult and out of control. I turned my back on my education, I refused to learn, and I had no respect for most people. All I can say is that I now realize that all teenagers need recognition, admiration, and a sense of belonging—not just from their families, but also from their peers. I had gotten that comforting sense in Indianapolis, just by being myself. In Miami, I had to fight to fit in, as well as to protect myself from being attacked. But here in Vineland, I felt like I had to

Vineland High School

make the first move as the rebellious new kid who wouldn't let anyone bully or best him. That was my "brand." I was proud of my reputation.

During my middle school and high school years, my academic work was disappointing, to say the least. I wasn't focused on my schoolwork, and I was in trouble most of the time. It didn't help that I felt demeaned and segregated when the school slotted me into its English as a Second Language Program. Right or wrong, I believed that the American students viewed the ESL group as mentally inferior, and that made me feel insecure around them. I cut myself off from them, and instead I hung out exclusively with the Spanish kids. This short-sighted move kept me out of extra-curricular activities where I might have met a broader group of friends. The memory of my popularity during my short stay in Indianapolis haunted me. Despite my limited English skills, I'd been friends with everyone there.

Vineland High School

My solution to my frustrating social position was to act out. I became a bully to get the attention I craved. This behavior often led me straight to the principal's office. I wasn't afraid to use the boxing skills I'd learned in Spain to challenge the toughest kids in school, until I learned the hard way one day that I wasn't invincible. It took almost getting killed in a fight with the captain of the wrestling team to make me realize that I was on the road to nowhere.

I don't remember how that violent fight started, but I do know that I initiated it. My opponent was huge—way bigger and stronger than me. He slammed his meaty fist into my face, breaking my nose and making me bleed furiously. Next thing I knew, he had his arm around my neck in a chokehold, and I struggled for breath. A minute or so more of that, and I'd have been gone.

I remember my mother being called into the principal's office and having to sit there in silence. She was clearly mortified. She couldn't speak English well enough to talk to the principal, so she didn't understand what had happened. All she knew was that somehow her beloved son had dishonored the family, and her disappointment in me at that moment was boundless.

My mother told me that if I didn't stop fighting and start concentrating on my schoolwork, I could kiss my future goodbye. Meanwhile, my father continued to believe in me and support me, telling me what a great engineer I'd become someday and reminding me how smart I was. He called me *campeón*—Spanish for champion.

That was all it took for me to have a life-changing revelation. I vowed to put my fighting days behind me. Never again would I allow myself to get into a situation that would hurt my parents—especially my mother. From then on, I managed my temper. I dropped that chip from my shoulder, and I focused on being the kind of son my hard-working parents deserved—the kind of son who would be worthy of all the sacrifices they had made to give him a better life.

Work—and My Father—Saved Me

My parents' belief in me helped me overcome my demons, and my father modeled the behavior he expected from me by having me work alongside him.

It was a habit we'd started when I was a little boy in Cárdenas, me tagging along to my father's job and his carpentry shop. We continued that bond in Miami, where I helped him paint new apartments under construction. He taught me the right way to hold paint brushes and rollers, and how to properly clean the tools at the end of the day. In Vineland, I became his assistant as he worked his side job as a handyman. I learned carpentry, plumbing, and electrical maintenance mostly by just watching him.

One thing my father drilled into me was the importance of safety. He had lost a finger when he got distracted while working in his carpentry shop in Cuba. At the time, I took his strictness and carefulness as being too protective of me. It used to annoy me that that he wouldn't let me handle the power tools, so I complained that I wanted to learn how to use them. I didn't want to just be his assistant.

But my father told me that a good assistant knew as much as the master by learning the proper sequence of the work. He taught me to know the right moment to hand him the tools and materials he needed without him having to ask me for them— sort of like the scrub nurse's relationship to the surgeon in the operating room. He taught me how to be more efficient while I worked by always putting the tools away in the same spot so that I didn't

My parents' house in Vineland, New Jersey

waste time looking for them.

Even though my anger faded over time, and I stopped acting out so much, school was still difficult for me. It didn't help that my parents still couldn't speak or understand much English, so they couldn't help me with my schoolwork. Their lack of English language skills and their necessary focus on working and feeding the family also meant that they couldn't talk to my teachers or participate in any parental school activities.

Looking back, I realize that our Miami experience—when we were so desperately poor—had been terrifying for my parents. That awful memory made them focus all their energies on our financial survival in Vineland. Succeeding in their jobs now took precedence over other things, such as improving their English or helping me with my schoolwork.

But they never stopped beating the drum for me to attend college. My earning a college degree was paramount to them both, and it created an expectation in me that I knew I had to fulfill. My mother wanted me to become an engineer because she knew I was good in math and science. I did well in those subjects and always had. She told me that math was a universal language, and she promised that even as a clumsy English speaker I could excel.

Being the wise woman she was, my mother knew better than I did where my talents lay. One sign was how serious I was about building bridges, roads, and buildings out of my wooden blocks in Cuba when I was a little boy. It wasn't just play for me. As I built, I was envisioning how the buildings would work and how people would use the roads. She also saw that I was much stronger academically in my math and science classes than in anything else, and she knew that strength in those sciences was an important quality for any engineer.

As a parent, one of your jobs is to understand your child's gifts and then encourage them to find a career that welcomes them. When your child's talents are a good match for their career, it helps ensure their success. Both my parents believed that an engineering career would allow me to put my skills to good use.

Unfortunately, by high school I had done my best—certainly without meaning to—to torpedo my parents' expectations. Throughout my scholastic career, my grades were low, my grasp of English was still iffy, and my attitude was so bad that I frequently found myself in the principal's office. When I met with my guidance counselor in my junior year to discuss my future, he asked me what my ambitions were. When I told him my dream was to become an engineer, he scoffed at me because my grades were so low.

Sometimes, the very best motivation you can receive is having someone tell you NO. For me, that motivating kick in the pants came that day with my guidance counselor all but laughed in my face. He told me I wasn't college material and that I should abandon the notion of becoming an engineer. Vocational school would be my best shot at a higher education, in his opinion.

That did it for me. His less than enthusiastic view of my future made me vow to prove him wrong. Bottom line, I refused to let my guidance counselor derail my dreams—or the expectations my parents had set for me.

That meeting became another magic moment in my life, another major turning point. My guidance counselor's opinion of me certainly stung, but instead of letting it kill my spirit or anger me, it ignited my need to prove him wrong by becoming an engineer.

CHAPTER 6

BECOMING AN ENGINEER

After that fateful meeting with my guidance counselor in my junior year, I took stock of myself. I got real about what I needed to do to make my ambition of becoming an engineer a reality. Though I managed to graduate from high school, my GPA wasn't as high as I needed it to be. I knew that I needed to both boost my grades and become fluent in speaking, reading, and writing English if I had any hope of being accepted to an engineering school.

I decided I could accomplish that goal if I attended Cumberland County Community College for two years. Once I enrolled, I focused strictly on my studies, and I graduated with decent grades and an associate degree.

I excelled in math and science at CCCC, and my professor asked me if I could tutor students who needed extra help. That recognition was all I needed to rededicate myself to getting top grades. If I didn't ace an A on an exam, I'd be unhappy with myself.

Still, I struggled a bit in other courses which depended on a better mastery of English. There, my rebel attitude bubbled up when I asked the professor why it was so important that I understand the meaning of, say, a Shakespeare play. My professor had to be extra-patient when explaining Shakespearian language to me.

Happily though, I discovered as I progressed that most engineers will never need to understand the inner meaning of King Lear, as long as they have an understanding of the intricacies of algebra, calculus, trigonometry, geometry, chemistry, physics, biology, and computer sciences.

And it also turned out that my parents had been right all along: I would excel as an engineer.

After graduation, I applied to several New Jersey state colleges that offered engineering programs. I was ecstatic when Rutgers University School of Engineering accepted me, and I was even more over the moon when I learned that my hard work in community college qualified me for student loans and grants. Funding my education by myself was a necessity because my parents couldn't afford Rutgers' tuition.

Life in New Brunswick

Because Rutgers was a nearly two-hour drive from Vineland, I lived on campus my first year. I got married in the summer shortly after my first year there. Today, it's rare for kids to get married before they graduate from college. But for me, being married in college actually made me more focused on my schoolwork.

Remember Silvia from *Liceo Cubano,* my Cuban youth group meetings?

I still remember her as a blond, hazel-eyed girl with very curly hair. She would sit on a sofa throwing occasional glances my way as I sat on the floor listening to my cousin Elbi lead the group. At the time, I was 14 and Silvia was 12.

We became fast friends from the moment we met. We called each other pet names. She called me Dumbo because of my huge ears. (Thankfully, my head eventually grew in proportion to them.) My father told me that big ears were a sign of intelligence.

That boosted my confidence, so I didn't mind Silvia's gentle teasing, and any self-confidence issues I had about my ears faded away.

In retaliation for calling me Dumbo, I called her Bozo because of her curly hair. Later on in our lives, our nicknames for each other became a story we told and retold to our children and friends, as we remembered those sweet early days when our love for each other first flowered.

Silvia's family was also from Cárdenas and had immigrated to the United States in the early sixties. After living in Miami and Tampa, they eventually settled in Vineland where they had relatives. Silvia was just three years old when she left Cuba and she adapted quickly to her new surroundings. As an adult, she spoke both Spanish and English without an accent—although she came to this country at a very young age, she never lost her Cuban heritage. In fact, people would say that she spoke more like a Cuban than I did. She was a great example of how you can assimilate into another culture without leaving your heritage behind.

Over time, our relationship evolved from a very close friendship to a flourishing romance. I remember our first kiss. We were hiding on the side of the apartment complex where our families lived. Silvia told me that she was going on a vacation to see her family in Indianapolis, Indiana, where my Aunt Belinda and Uncle Amado still lived. She told me that she would visit them for me and that she'd miss me while she was away. When she told she'd be gone for several days, I didn't want her to leave. I realized my feelings for Silvia had graduated from friendship to love.

So at first as friends, then as romantic partners, we were together from the time we met. Before we got married, we attended different schools. While I was in my first year at Rutgers College of Engineering, she attended Glassboro State University where she was working on her teaching and math degrees.

During my first year in college, I didn't have a car. Silvia's mother, Olga, would take her to visit me on campus or pick me up sometimes on a Friday so that I could spend the weekend in Vineland with my parents and friends. Olga was like another mother to me. She was always very sweet and loving, and I felt very comfortable with her.

On August 6, 1977, Silvia and I married in Sacred Heart Church in Vineland, New Jersey. Silvia applied

Our wedding on August 6, 1977

to Rutgers University, and she was accepted to continue her math studies there in September. During our married student life, we lived with Silvia's mother, Olga in her Vineland apartment when we were off school during the summers. During the school year, we studied, but in the summers, Silvia and I each worked two jobs while we lived with her mother, saving all our money so that we could concentrate on our studies during the school year.

After we got married and returned to college in September, we moved into Rutgers' housing for married students. We didn't have much—no furniture, no car. On our first night in the school apartment, we slept on a discarded mattress we'd found that we wrapped in a plastic cover. We started to furnish the apartment with furniture Silvia's uncle had in his basement, and we decorated our place with tall, dried grasses we cut at a nearby pond. We had a battery-operated radio for entertainment, and we'd only listen to it at night after we finished studying. We were study fanatics—partly due to our ambition, and partly because we couldn't afford a TV or any other activities.

I believe that coming from very similar backgrounds and sharing common goals is helpful in adjusting to married life. Although we married very young, we did not miss the normal dating life which most American teenagers and young adults experience. In Cuban culture, at least back then, your parents didn't expect you to date a lot—most parents were quite protective of their daughters. Though young men had more leeway to date around, I didn't really take advantage of it. Once I met my Silvia, that was it for me.

The Challenges of Engineering School

Despite my commitment and hard work, my first semester in engineering school was challenging. I wasn't used to learning in those large auditorium classrooms where the professors seemed like disembodied voices. I was still having difficulties with the language and I had to use an English-to-Spanish technical dictionary to translate terms I didn't understand. As a result, I flunked my first physics exam.

Nelson Alberto Diaz

Rutgers University yearbook photo

During my first year at Rutgers, I lived in the dorms at Livingston College and had to take a short bus ride to the Rutgers college campus in New Brunswick. A lot of the general basic classes, like physics, were held at the Rutgers college campus.

After the physics professor returned my exam with an "F," I was miserable and furious with myself. I took the bus back to the dorm and spent the trip looking out the window so that others couldn't see me cry. My mind raced with depressing thoughts: Am I really college material? Is engineering right for me? Do I need this pressure? Maybe I should give up and get a job that doesn't need a college degree. Then came the most depressing thought of all: What am I going to tell my parents when I go visit them this weekend?

I went off to see my parents and Silvia with my tail between my legs. In tears, I cried to my father that engineering school was too hard, and that I didn't think I was going to make it. Despite the fact that I was almost as big as he was at this point, my father hugged me and sat me on his lap. I still remember his words of encouragement as he told me, "*Campeón,* you will get used to it. Just don't give up, study harder, and you will pass your next exam."

I guess his encouragement was all I needed, because that's exactly what happened. I made it a point to seek out, befriend, and study with students who were at the top of the class. I remember studying physics and calculus with two brothers from Puerto Rico, Carlos and Felipe. Carlos was a pre-med student and Felipe was studying physics and mathematics. We studied almost every evening after dinner at the campus cafeteria. This became my routine during my first year at Rutgers while I lived in the dorms.

I loved Calculus classes and did extremely well in them. When I took my first engineering classes in Statics and Dynamics, which are requirements for all engineers, I knew then that my focus would be the field of Civil Engineering. I would be able to turn my childhood games of building roads, bridges, and structures into reality. My hard work paid off, and I graduated Rutgers School of Engineering with a B+ average. I still regret that I missed getting honors by just a few decimal points.

My Rutgers graduation

After successfully finishing my first year at Rutgers University, I started my second year as a married student. Silvia and I lived in the college's married student housing dorm and dedicated ourselves to school. We studied together most evenings and drilled ourselves with questions the night before an exam. Being married and leaving behind the dorm scene helped me sharpen my focus on my studies.

In my second year at Rutgers, most of the classes were more specific to the Civil Engineering program. I continue to befriend classmates that I considered to be at the top of the class. Two of them, Marcelo and Larry, were my best friends after Silvia and I moved to Rutgers. Marcelo was also married, and eventually took an apartment in the married students' dorms. We lived across the hall from each other and spent time studying as well as socializing together. Marcelo, Larry, and I studied together all the time.

In class we were friendly rivals, vying for the best grades. I remember how happy I'd be when my grade beat theirs on

Silvia's Rutgers graduation

an exam. Here was another lesson I learned from my father, who used to tell me to hang around people who would help me move up, not those who would drag me down.

I was told I couldn't make it

My Early Engineering Career

After I graduated from engineering school in 1979, I started looking for a job as a civil engineer. Unfortunately, my timing couldn't have been worse. The country was in the middle of a global oil crisis, triggered in part by the Iranian revolution. We were experiencing the most severe recession since World War II, but no matter what, I had to find a job. Silvia helped me write dozens and dozens of cover letters, and we sent my resume to as many companies as we could find.

It's hard to describe just how different job hunting was 40 years ago than it is today. Now, applying for a position is a fairly streamlined, it's a cut-and-paste process thanks to computers and email. But back then, it was a lot of legwork. You'd have to go through phonebooks or even to the library to find lists of appropriate companies, copy down names and numbers, phone each company to find the right person to send the resume to, and then send each prospect an original hand-typed letter to go with the resume. My wife dove into job-hunting and spent hours at the typewriter pounding out letters.

Finally, I landed an interview with a small company, Design and Project Engineers, and nailed the job right away. It was a start-up business owned by two brothers from New Brunswick. One brother ran the company, and the other did the field work. I was their first hire.

It turned out to be the perfect launching pad for my career. The owner, Robert (Bob) Parcells, became a mentor to me, and our

My first job

friendship lasted long after he had to close the business several years later. I had his total confidence. In fact, he had more confidence in me than I had in myself. He gave me assignments I didn't feel prepared to handle, which made me a little nervous. I remember the first structure that I designed for a chemical company. I would deliberately pass by it every so often to assure myself that the building was still standing.

Bob always reviewed my projects, and discussed with me different ideas to improve my work and perhaps find ways to make the overall design more efficient and less expensive. He believed in me and in my abilities. Because it was such a small company, I got to experience all aspects of the business, from doing office work, to billing, to writing up proposals. I even took clients out for lunch to discuss their plans. Bob exposed me to everything. It was a great way for an ambitious young man like me to start out.

Soon, the company began to grow, and Bob decided to bring on a general manager. After several months, things between the new manager and Bob weren't working out and he was fired. I saw my opportunity and told Bob that I'd like a shot at the general manager's job. His immediate response was, "You're too young."

"Haven't I been able to accomplish everything that you've asked of me?"

My mentor Bob Purcell and me

I responded. He thought for a moment and said yes.

I told him I'd make him a deal. "You don't have to give me a raise. Just give me the job. Try me for six months, and if I do the job well, then we can talk."

He said he'd think about it. That evening, as I was home with Silvia, Bob called right before dinner. "Nelson, I thought about what you said. You're the new general manager. And guess what? You can't work as the general manager at your current salary. I'm going to double it, and I'm going to give you the car we bought for Russ."

In the blink of an eye, I'd gone from junior engineer to general manager. After I hung up the phone, I told Silvia, "Don't cook. We're going out to eat. We've got money now!"

In time, I became almost like a son to Bob. Silvia and I would visit him at his beach house on the Jersey shore, and we were quite close. It was the perfect first job. I was able to design as well as to be a field supervisor when needed. I was

One of the job sites I managed

involved in every aspect of a project from design work to supervising the building of a structure. It was great to have the opportunity to see a project all the way through. If I'd gotten a job at one of the bigger engineering firms, I'd probably have ended up in cubicle and never gotten the perspective of being involved in a total project from start to finish.

Worldwide Recession Alters My Dreams

Despite my personal and professional success at Design and Project Engineers, the country's economy was still in shambles. Clients were putting their capital improvement projects on hold, and the fallout from that meant that our firm couldn't survive the shock. Bob met with me to let me know that he'd made the painful decision to close the company.

We prepared for what was going to happen. One day, he asked me whether I'd started looking for a new job. I told him I hadn't. He said, "Why not? You know what our plan is."

"I want to be with you 100 percent until the very last day," I told him. And that's exactly what I did. I didn't apply for a new job until we'd closed the doors to the business. At that point, I'd been with the company for about three years.

It wasn't an easy time for us. Silvia was pregnant and had started maternity leave, and I was unemployed. It was the summer of 1982. I applied to every job I could find, and again Silvia typed up my resume and cover letters. I probably sent that resume out to 100 companies or so. But nobody seemed to be hiring because companies were all putting their building projects on the back burner.

Becoming an Investor

During my time in New Brunswick and working for Design and Project Engineers, I befriended one of the welders while I was working in the field during one of the projects. He told me that he'd started investing in real estate, and about the tax benefits and

Working on our first investment house

cash flow generated by the rents he was collecting. I listened to him intently and asked many questions. I decided if he could do it, I could too. I became a part-time real estate investor.

Without an engineering job or any prospects, this could become my way to provide for my family. So, I decided to use the money we'd saved to continue to invest in real estate. Silvia and I embarked on an investment journey that would become my second career.

While I was working in Design and Project Engineers and Silvia had her first teaching job, we bought our first investment property. Silvia and I renovated it and sold it a year later. Although the mortgage interest was a whopping 17 percent, we made more money flipping that property than I had in a year as an engineer! I was hooked. Since the job market was so slow, I decided to forge my own path in real estate. After all, I had all those essential skills I'd learned at my father's knee—carpentry, plumbing, tiling, and electrical work.

While everything was falling into place for Silvia and I, we received a call from my sister in Vineland. Sadly, we lost my mother to a heart attack, suddenly and prematurely, while Silvia was still pregnant with our first son. My mother was only 49, and it broke my heart that she never got to meet her first grandchild.

After we sold the property in New Brunswick, we moved back to Vineland, while I continued to search for an engineering job.

Silvia and I ended up using all our savings to buy properties, with her backing me 100

With Julio, Rosa, and Silvia on a Caribbean cruise

percent. She never worried (at least not out loud to me), even though I was digging deep into our savings at a time when we were both out of work. It boosted my confidence to know that she trusted me so completely.

While in Vineland, Silvia and I reconnected with our friends there. One of our friends, Julio who was like brother to Silvia and me, had married Rosa. Rosa and Julio were also part of that Cuban youth group who spent countless hours playing and swimming at the apartment complex pool. Julio had also gone to Rutgers, where he earned a law degree. After passing the bar, he worked in a law firm in Vineland.

Julio and I have always been great friends. To this

day, we spend hours talking about everything under the sun, including real estate. During one of those discussions, the idea of investing together came up. We were a good fit: Julio understood all the legal aspects of real estate and had many connections in Vineland where he practiced law. I had the construction knowledge and could assess a property's renovation needs, estimate cost, and could even do the work myself.

Rosa was also one of Silvia's best friends and we became a team: Silvia and me, Rosa and Julio. All of us pitched in to renovate the properties we'd purchased. I was responsible for the renovation work, and Julio did the legal part as well as looking for properties and helping me during the renovation. Silvia and Rosa painted and cleaned the properties as we'd work to find a buyer. Each couple invested $2,500 for a total of $5,000 and that's how our investment company started. Our partnership was called NJD Enterprises. I can't remember how many homes we flipped together in Vineland—it was quite a few—at a time when flipping wasn't as common as it is now.

Even as we worked on renovating the properties we purchased, I was sending out resumes to every engineering firm I could find. Around the time our first son Nelson Luis was born on September 25, 1982, I finally received the good news from one of the jobs to which I had applied. Pennsylvania Power and Light in Allentown, Pennsylvania wanted to interview me for a job in their Nuclear Department.

I had my first interview over the phone with one of the human resource managers. Shortly after that first interview, they called me in for a face-to-face interview. I remember driving to Allentown for that interview and telling myself to relax and do the best I could. After the interview, I had to stop the car and actually threw up on the shoulder of Route 22. I guess you could say that the stress of the day had gotten to me.

To my amazement, I got the job. This would mean a move for my family, and we had to figure out what to do about our business in New Jersey. It was clear after just a few months that I wouldn't be able to manage our properties in Vineland, so all four of us partners decided it was time to sell. After the proper-ties were sold, Julio used his share of the profits to open his own law practice. I used our share to invest in proper-ties in Allentown.

My professional engineer license in Pennsylvania

ALLENTOWN, PENNSYLVANIA

CHAPTER 8

THE LEHIGH VALLEY WELCOMES THE DIAZ FAMILY

With the prospect of my exciting new job in hand—I would be an instrumental part of helping PPL build its first nuclear power plant—Silvia and I and our baby, Nelson, moved into the comfortable three-bedroom colonial home we bought on Calvary Avenue in Emmaus. As we settled in, we were surprised to discover that we seemed to be the only Hispanic family for miles around. One clue was that we were the only Diaz listed in the phone book—that would be like finding only one listing for Jones or Smith. The other clue was that even basic Spanish food products weren't available at our local grocery store. The

Our first home in Emmaus, Pennsylvania

nearest place to shop for my espresso coffee or Goya foods was several miles away in Allentown.

I'd talk to Silvia about my fears that people wouldn't welcome us, or that they'd find ways to express their discomfort at suddenly having Hispanic neighbors. Silvia would just shake her head and tell me that we had nothing to worry about. She was a people person. On nice days, we'd take our lawn chairs and sit in our new driveway and greet our neighbors. Pretty soon, we were putting out extra chairs and folks would stop by to visit. Silvia would brew up some Cuban coffee, and we'd make new friends. Her personality was so warm that no one could resist her. Our home became a magnet for our neighbors, who dropped by often just to have a sip of the delicious

Cuban espresso coffee that Silvia made for them.

Even as we settled into our home and neighborhood, we were driving back and forth to Vineland most weekends. My father and Silvia's mother, sister Lourdes, and aunts still lived there, as did my younger brother and sister. My best friend and partner, Julio, and his wife, Rosa, were also there with their two kids. We all tried to keep our extended family together as best we could, now that nearly 100 miles separated us.

Soon, we welcomed two more sons into our family. In 1984, Philip came along, and our son Daniel was born in 1985. But along with the births of our sons would come heartbreak. Shortly after Daniel was born, we lost my father, also prematurely and from a heart attack. He was just 58.

Now that I'd lost both my parents, I became head of the Diaz family and assumed responsibility for my brother and sister. I made sure that

Silvia and I and our three sons

my sister finished college at Drexel University and that both my siblings had everything they needed.

As our boys grew, so did their school and extracurricular activities. Pretty soon, there was always a soccer game or two on the weekends, and our trips to Vineland lessened as we focused on raising our growing family in Emmaus.

Though neither Silvia nor I were "helicopter parents" by any means, we did encourage all three of our boys to get involved with activities they enjoyed. As a result, they were on baseball, soccer, wrestling, football, and swimming teams.

We also encouraged them to play musical instruments. Nelson played the drums and was a member of the Emmaus High School band, Philip took saxophone lessons, and Daniel played the violin. Just as my parents before me, we were attentive to their abilities

With Silvia, our sons, and our first grandson, Nelson

and pushed them to pursue activities that interested them—activities in which they had abilities that would help them succeed.

One afternoon, as we sat at the Emmaus McDonald's with our sons, a bus parked nearby us. It was filled with what appeared to be members of a Black congregation church. Daniel, who was always very inquisitive and also a non-stop talker, said "Papi, those people are brown." I was very surprised by his comment and tried to explain to him and his brothers that there were people of other races that looked different than us.

As I mentioned, when we first moved to Emmaus, our family was the only Hispanic family we knew of, and there were very few, if any, other families of color.

After we arrived home, I talked with Silvia about Daniel's remark, and told her that I thought we needed to expose our children to more diversity. Mutually, we agreed to find ways to do that. My idea was to send them to the Boys and Girls Club of Allentown during their summer breaks. They attended the club, located in Allentown's multicultural city center, for several summers. There, they interacted with children of other races and soon had many friends. They quickly learned not to judge others by their skin color or physical attributes.

Our children made Silvia and I extremely proud.

They have grown to be great men, each successful in their own way and completely independent. Silvia and I think of them as our life's masterpieces.

As I went through my life story in my mind before I sat down to write this book, it occurred to me that one thing that remained constant was how important our family was, and how proud we were to pass along the family traditions to the next generation. For example, I remember the loving examples my grandparents set for me, taking me on those long motorcycle rides to the beach. I remember that our first home in Cuba was with my mother's parents, and I remember how involved they were in our lives and how my parents welcomed their influence on us.

Now, when I look at my grandchildren, Nelson and Victor, they have a lot of the same interests I had

My grandchildren

as a boy—and I also see that they love to build things, just as I did. Together they carry my father's name Nelson Victor.

My grandchildren love coming to my house and hanging out with me, just as I did with my grandfather. It's a very sweet point in life when you can recognize loving patterns repeating themselves.

When I lived with my Aunt Belinda in Indianapolis, I learned how important it is to become immersed in your new culture. She was wise to invest in intensive English language sessions for me, even though it took several years for me to become truly bi-lingual. When we had our son, Nelson, Silvia and I thought we would be doing him a favor by raising him to speak Spanish during his toddler years, figuring that English would come easily to him once he started school.

But instead of putting him ahead, speaking only Spanish actually held him back a bit, as we learned at our first parent-teacher conference. Nelson's teacher told us that he was a little below average—something no parent ever wants to hear. She thought it was because we were confusing him by only speaking to him in Spanish.

We immediately took her advice and began speaking English at home—and looking back, I think that could have been a mistake on our parts. Eventually,

Nelson would have gotten to the point where he could have spoken both languages fluently.

Now my sons and I recognize the importance of knowing several languages and recognize that you can assimilate into a new culture without giving up on your own. We all make an effort to talk Spanish to my grandchildren and even their wives try to learn as well.

For me it's a great pleasure to see how my sons and their new families enjoy my Cuban heritage. They love the food, music, dancing, and our very lively parties.

Helping Construct an Eco-Friendly Nuclear Power for the Lehigh Valley

Some 50 years ago, PPL took a forward-thinking approach to developing nuclear power as a clean energy source to serve their customers. Their first project was the Susquehanna Steam Electric station near Berwick, PA.

The project was nearing completion when PPL hired me as a Cost and Scheduling Engineer in 1982, though several months would pass until I could actually start working. I first had to become a U.S. citizen, and because I was working in a nuclear facility, I also had to pass a security clearance. Once I'd accomplished both those tasks, I stepped into the job.

I would be responsible for keeping the project on schedule—and on budget, which is no small feat for building a nuclear power plant. This was a complicated, expensive project with lots of moving parts, and the longer a project like that takes, the more expensive it becomes. I had to oversee countless details and make sure all the aspects of the job were properly completed. The station's first unit went into service in June 1983 with a second unit following in February of 1985.

Although I enjoyed my job, I realized early on that it didn't provide me with the same satisfaction I'd enjoyed when I was buying properties, fixing them up, and selling them at a nice profit. So, I decided to carry on the tradition my father began. He'd always had two jobs—one that provided a measure of financial security for his family and a second one that satisfied his need to build things. His greatest gift to me was the lessons he taught me in his carpentry shop in Cuba when I was a little boy, later in Miami, and then in Vineland. I knew how to build, paint, install flooring,

One of my buildings in Allentown

wire for electricity, and make sure a structure was sound. Not only had my father taught me the "how to" of all these skills, he also taught me how to enjoy performing the tasks at hand and how to take pleasure in a job well done. These were powerful gifts that would last my lifetime.

Because I had already enjoyed success at being a real estate "flipper" in Vineland, I figured I could continue doing that in Allentown, the city close to Emmaus that Billy Joel immortalized in his famous song. Allentown, once a thriving metropolis thanks to its local industries, had fallen on hard times. Many of its houses in less desirable neighborhoods were in serious need of repair and of new owners committed to improving the community.

Long-Range Planning Leads to Success

My training as an engineer taught me the importance of planning and of committing plans

Celebrating my 50th birthday in St. Martin

to spreadsheets so that I could track the progress of a particular project. Because this process worked so well for my projects at PPL, I figured it would also work for my extracurricular real estate projects.

First, I set a goal: I would retire from PPL at the age of 55. I created a long-range plan to achieve that goal, which included knowing how much my net worth would have to be when I turned 55 so that my family could maintain our comfortable lifestyle. I also knew how much I'd have to earn every year, both from my PPL salary and from the proceeds from my real estate work, in order to live well after I quit PPL. To make sure I was on track, I'd review my spreadsheet every few months.

All my discipline and hard work paid off, and I was able to meet my goal early. I resigned from PPL exactly 20 years, nearly to the day, after I'd started there. I was now a full-time real estate entrepreneur.

When I look back, I have to wonder where that discipline and drive came from. Although my father worked very hard to get our family out of Cuba and to save me from the draft, he was always focused on his immediate need to provide for his family. For him, success meant being able to live in a safe neighborhood and to provide security and a comfortable life for us all. That was what success looked like to him.

As luck would have it, at about the same time I decided that building wealth was important to me, PPL offered its executives a seminar by Franklin Covey, called *7 Habits of Highly Successful People*. It was based on the best-selling book by Stephen R. Covey. In the 1980s, countless companies offered *7 Habits* seminars to their employees.

7 Habits taught me how to create and set goals and helped me develop the ability to put a plan together for my life. To take it one step further, I also attended a Tony Robbins seminar and learned his secrets for maximizing my professional performance.

One thing I learned from this work is that it's easy to create goals. Everyone has goals, like "I want to be a millionaire," for example. But to be successful, I learned, you have to have a detailed plan for how to get there. That's why my spreadsheets and the lessons I learned in those seminars became so important to my success. I knew how much money I would need to save every year so that I could accumulate enough wealth to reach my goal of an early retirement.

I also believe that those early days living with my parents in Miami and Vineland, where we lacked many basic needs, influenced me in wanting to live better and be much more comfortable.

The Discipline of Saving

I latched onto a strategy early in my planning: I decided to never spend my raises. Each year at PPL, I would get a raise, and when I got promoted to project manager, I got an even bigger one. I never mentioned these raises to Silvia. I just added the extra money to our savings. In fact, I remember once Silvia asking me, "Why don't you ever get a raise?" And I replied, "Why, is there something missing? Something you need?" She looked at me and she understood that we had enough to run the house, and enough to feed and clothe everyone in the family. We weren't doing without. We just didn't go wild spending money on unnecessary items. Who needed a fancy car? That was fine with Silvia.

Because of my earnings, Silvia didn't have to work when the boys were little. She could stay home and take care of them, which was her preference. So, we didn't need daycare or babysitters. In fact, when we went out to dinner, we went as a family, and from that our sons learned how to behave well in company. We also took great family vacations, including a memorable road trip all the way to San Antonio. As a result, to this day, my three boys are very close to each other.

ALLENTOWN,
PENNSYLVANIA

CHAPTER 9

HELPING RENTERS BECOME HOMEOWNERS

I had made a life decision, and I created a plan to realize it. By day, I would be a Cost and Scheduling Engineer for PP&L. After work, I would continue my business of buying multi-family homes in the Allentown area, renovating them, and then renting out the apartments. Over time, though, I realized that eventually, I would lose my best tenants because they wanted to purchase homes of their own.

So, I thought, "What if I start buying single-family homes, fix them up, and then *sell* them to my tenants?" I might lose a tenant, but I'd gain a buyer.

To accomplish this, I knew had to have a really good team to work with. I needed a good mortgage broker, a realtor with excellent Allentown connections, and a lawyer. I also needed to understand all the government programs available to first-time home buyers.

I created a support structure for potential home buyers. My first step in working with my tenants was to have them fill out a questionnaire. One question asks, "If you had the opportunity to buy a house, describe the features you'd want it to have." That would help me pinpoint properties that would suit their needs.

I focused on potential buyers who were Hispanic because they trusted me, we spoke the same language, and I understood their culture. I would talk

to these hopeful homeowners about their finances and about what they wanted in a new home. Then, I'd send them to my mortgage broker, who could help them repair their credit if necessary. Finally, I'd go out scouting potential homes

My good friend and investment partner Ortelio

My never-ending project:
my Allentown home

with my trusted real estate broker, who understood what I was looking for, who knew the area and, perhaps most importantly, had the right connections.

My broker was key to helping me find promising properties. He taught me an important lesson: You make the money in real estate when you buy, not when you sell. If you don't buy right, he told me, you'll never make any money.

This all-important lesson means that it doesn't matter how much money you invest into improving a property, if it's the wrong property, it won't be profitable. And so, I had a certain profile for a potential house, and he knew that once I finished renovating it, we would all come out ahead. Together, my broker and I would find a fixer-upper that could meet my clients' needs.

So, what makes the "right" property? It's actually an equation. It is partly the property and its location, and it needs to meet a client's specific needs. Because I was focused on serving the Hispanic community that I knew and was close to, I concentrated on purchasing properties that my clients could afford. I was also keenly aware of what they needed and wanted in a house.

Once I had the buyer lined up, and a suitable potential property in mind for them, I would connect them with my mortgage broker. The mortgage broker would analyze the buyer's financial situation and say, "Well, you can buy if you do this and this and this," or "This

From tenants to owners

couple is ready to buy." Or sometimes, we learned that the buyer wasn't in the financial position to become an owner yet and would have to take certain steps to rebuild their credit and savings while they continued to rent. They might be disappointed to delay their home ownership journey for a while, but

Clients closing on one of the properties

they would walk away with a solid financial plan that could get them back on equal footing.

Another essential member of my team is my lawyer, who makes sure that all the paperwork—from contracts to mortgage agreements to deeds—is in perfect shape. A simple mistake in the paper-work—an incorrect date or name, for instance—can sink the entire project.

In my business, I also had to research and under-stand the many financial programs available to

A radio broadcasting station I remodeled in East Providence, Rhode Island

first-time and lower income home buyers. I got my tenants ready to be buyers by educating them about which of these programs was right for them. Then, I'd send them to work with my mortgage broker to fix whatever credit issues they had. I also sent them to seminars for first-time homebuyers.

It gives me immense satisfaction to know that I've been able to help turn people's lives around. I knew who my good tenants were, and I told myself, "I may lose them as renters eventually. Let me give them the opportunity to become owners and I will work with them to prepare them."

Becoming a homeowner gives people a stake in their neighborhood that they didn't have when they were tenants, and this has a positive ripple effect on an entire community. Now, instead of having a neighborhood of mostly renters, you have a neighborhood of proud homeowners who take responsibility for their homes and their streets. As a result, entire neighborhoods start becoming safer, better places to live—places where people can raise their families.

For me, my focus continues to be on building a strong family, just as my parents taught me. The lesson, which I'd learned from childhood, was that having a loyal, strong family is the key to living a happy, fulfilling, successful life. My parents sacrificed so much for us, and I can tell you that it was worth the investment they made. Giving the same attention to my own family became my life's work, and now I am able to help other people create strong families, too.

In fact, to a certain extent, I feel as if I have a familial connection with my buyers and tenants. Some people have suggested that I'm almost like an uncle who shares his wisdom and helps protect them as they work their way up to becoming homeowners.

Many times, after my new homeowners moved

into a house I've renovated for them, Silvia and I were the first guests invited for dinner. The word spread that Nelson Diaz was a guy who could help renters become owners. As I've said, the Hispanic community tends to be close, and good news travels fast.

Friends of new owners would say, "Oh my God, you bought a house. How do you do that?"

Their reply: "Well, let me connect you with the guy that helped us."

A Tribute to Silvia

I had finally reached the point in my life where I was exactly where I wanted to be. I had been able to retire from PPL as I'd planned, and my real business was booming. More important,

My beautiful wife, Silvia

my three sons were everything two parents could hope for: They were smart, productive, and kind, and they were starting to build their own families. I had come a long, long way from that little boy who had so many challenges thrown at him.

But then we got some terrible news about the pillar of my family and the source of its strength: my beautiful wife, Silvia. I've written of the many ways she helped and supported me and our family throughout our 44 years of marriage. In 2017, we learned that Silvia had pancreatic cancer—one of the deadliest cancers of all. One with no cure.

On that terrible day when we got the news of her diagnosis, she knew that she'd have a fight on her hands, and fight she did. I've never seen anyone with so much resolve and strength. Until that moment, I'd always thought of myself as the strong one in the family, but I realized that all along, Silvia had been the one whose strength kept our family going. She fought the disease bravely for three long years, and when she finally told me, "Hon, I'm ready to fly," I knew we had to let her go.

A few months before we lost her, my sons came to me with the idea of preserving one of Silvia's great legacies: Her Cuban family recipes, handed down over several generations. She loved the idea, and no matter how poorly she may have felt, she diligently wrote down the recipes by hand on file cards. My sons had them printed, and now one aspect of my Silvia will live on through the next generations.

Today, all my children are excellent cooks, and every time they prepare one of Silvia's recipes, it's almost like she's in the kitchen with them.

Although we enjoy all the dishes that Silvia prepared and that my children have mastered, Cuban flan was one of the favorites for our family and our friends. That Cuban desert was a classic that she would prepare every time there was a gathering in our house or in our friends' houses. I would like to share her recipe with you and challenge you to give it a try.

RECIPE FOR: Flan (Traditional - Cuban)   SERVES: 12
FROM: Silvia M. Diaz

*Carmel

Mix
1 can evaporated milk   { ½ cup sugar
1 can condensed milk   { 1 Tbsp water
6 eggs   { 1 squirt lemon
1 tsp vanilla
Pinch of Salt

In saucepan over med. heat, boil the *carmel ingredients to carmalize, light amber color. Pour into mold (flanera pan), swirl to coat the bottom and sides. Set aside.

→

- In blender, mix the eggs, milk, vanilla, and salt. Discard the frothed mix so mixture is smooth. Pour into carmalized pan, cover with foil. (or use flanera)
- Set into a larger pan for a water bath. Place in the middle oven rack. The water bath pan should have boiled water 2/3rd up the Flan pan.
- Cook in the oven 350° for an hour.
- Remove from water bath, chill in refrigerator.
- To serve, place flanera pan in hot water to soften the carmel. Turn pan upside down into another plate.   Enjoy!! :)

My son Daniel

My son Philip

My son Nelson

CHAPTER 10

SHARING MY LIFE'S LESSONS

My story is about a boy whose poor Cuban family found themselves on the wrong side of the Castro regime. Our experience proves that an immigrant family can succeed in this country despite starting out with very little.

I wrote this book because I knew my story could help inspire people. People who, like me, came here without speaking English, people who struggled in their homelands due to politics and poverty, people who came here seeking opportunities and a more hopeful future. My story is a real rags-to-riches saga.

Despite our poverty, I was rich, and had been since birth, in one all-important way: I always had the power of a strong, committed family behind me. My mother and father worked as a team to raise me and my siblings as free-thinking, independent people who always knew how much they were loved. From the time I was a little boy, my father's pet name for me was "*campeón,*" meaning champion.

Even though neither of my parents spoke much English or had much in the way of schooling, they knew that education would be the key to unlocking a brighter future for me. They believed in the importance of teaching me to be independent, to rely on myself, and not to wait for them to fix my problems. It wasn't always easy for them because I was a pretty wayward teen. Yet somehow, they knew just the right combination of strength and compassion to use to keep me on track. When I was at my most difficult, getting into bloody fights and nearly flunking out of high school, their support for me never wavered. Knowing that they believed in me was everything—it made me want to change my ways and earn their respect.

I'd like to take this opportunity to share some of the most important lessons I've learned.

A strong family is everything.

My parents taught me crucial life lessons about how to take care of myself—and then they'd step back and let me learn, even if that meant watching me make mistakes. I think their focus on teaching me how to be self-reliant prepared me for what was to come, because I was confident that I had the tools to handle pretty much any situation that came along. When my wife Silvia and I became parents, we took the same approach with our three sons, and they rewarded us by growing into fine young men—I am a very proud father.

At a recent Diaz family Thanksgiving, I was reminded of the importance of embracing family. Now that our sons have married and brought their wives and children into our family, we've expanded our Cuban culture to embrace Americans as well as Middle Easterners—it's not just me, Silvia, and the boys anymore. Now dishes like koshari and baklava join turkey, ham and Cuban rice and beans on our Thanksgiving table.

Brains beat brawn.

When I was sent away, alone, to Spain at the age of 13, I learned how to solve my own problems. I had many challenges to surmount and no adult around who could help me. I was bullied physically and emotionally, but I figured out how to defend myself with my fists as well as with my intellect. Over time and through many trials, I learned that there is always somebody stronger and that defending myself physically will only lead to trouble. Overcoming problems using my intelligence was a much smarter solution.

Don't listen to naysayers.

When my high school guidance counselor told me to focus on a vocational school instead of college, it became a major turning point for me. My parents— my mother, in particular—had always told me I was smart, and that a college education would ensure my future success. I knew my guidance counselor couldn't be right in thinking I wasn't college material. His put-down of me certainly stung, but instead of letting it kill my spirit or making me angry, it ignited a desire to prove him wrong. I would show him that I could get into college, succeed academically, and realize my dream of becoming an engineer.

Believe in your children.

My advice to parents is taken from the way my parents raised me. Through them, I learned that one of your jobs as a parent is to understand your child's gifts and then encourage them to find a career that uses those gifts. When your child's talents are a good match for their career, it helps ensure their success. Both my parents believed that an engineering career would allow me to put my math and science skills to good use. I believe that a parent's main responsibility is to help your children grow into independent adults.

Seek friends who set good examples.

My father used to tell me to hang around people who would help me move up, not those who would drag me down. So, when I decided to turn my life around in college—when I decided to succeed instead of fail—I made it a point to seek out and befriend smart, hard-working students. For example, in my Civil Engineering program at Rutgers, I befriended two of the top students in class, Marcelo and Larry. They became my best friends in college, and we studied together all the time. In class we saw each other as rivals, vying for the best grades. In a friendly but serious way, we competed with each other, and I remember how happy I'd be when my grade beat theirs on an exam. This competition pushed me to be the best.

Set goals—but create a plan to achieve them.

Everyone has goals, like "I want to be a millionaire," for example. But to be successful, I learned, you have to have a plan for how to get there. And that's why taking programs like *7 Habits of Highly Successful People* became so important to achieving my goals. I knew how much I would need to earn every year so that I could accumulate enough wealth to reach my goal of an early retirement. Without a detailed plan in place, you will find it difficult to attain your goals.

Use your time wisely.

Setting goals and creating a plan to achieve them will only come to fruition if you invest your time wisely. Prioritize your daily activities to support your plan. Many times during the day you may feel overwhelmed with issues and problems to solve. You may become frazzled by everything you may have on your plate, but having an orderly way to tackle them according to your priorities will help you focus and allow you to solve them efficiently.

I believe there is only one thing that you can never recover once it is gone: TIME.

Make your money when you buy.

I learned an important lesson from my real estate broker, who was key to helping me find promising properties. He said, "You make the money in real estate when you buy, not when you sell. If you don't buy right, you may never make any money."

Achieving success as a real estate investor.

First, you have to learn about what makes a property a good prospect for an investment. As I discovered, it's an equation that factors in partly the property and its location, along with a client's specific needs. Since in my career, I focused on serving the Hispanic community, I was also keenly aware of how much property my client could afford and what they needed and wanted in a house.

ACKNOWLEDGMENTS

My beautiful wife, Silvia, gave me the courage to make this book possible. Though her loss left me heartbroken, I hope readers will know that she lives on through me, our sons, and our grandchildren.

Heartfelt thanks go to my sons: Nelson; Philip and his wife, Shannon; and Daniel and his wife, Magan. They've been a bottomless well of strength and have supported me endlessly, digging up family photographs and sharing their memories.

I'd also like to thank the talented staff at Bright Communications, who helped me produce this book and made its birth such a gratifying project.

ABOUT THE AUTHOR

With the support of his family, Cuban-born Nelson A. Diaz escaped a certain fate as a soldier in Castro's army by emigrating to America—via Spain—when he was thirteen. Several years later, he graduated with an advanced degree in engineering from Rutgers University.

Today, Nelson is the founder/owner of Mi Casa Properties in Allentown, Pennsylvania. He and his team focus on acquiring, rehabilitating, and managing single, multi-family, and commercial properties in urban areas of Lehigh County. Nelson led Mi Casa while serving as a Project Manager in the Nuclear Department for PPL Electric Utilities, until his retirement from PPL a few years ago.

Nelson served on the Board of Directors of Sacred Heart Hospital, the Hispanic American Organization, and the Allentown Chamber of Commerce, and he was appointed to the Governor's Advisory Commission on Latino Affairs by Governors Corbett and Wolf. Nelson was awarded the "Good Turn Award" by the Minsi Trails Council Boy Scouts of America for establishing an educational partnership between PPL Electric Utilities and Allentown's inner-city schools.

The Mayor of Allentown selected Nelson to serve on the Board of Directors of Allentown Neighborhood Improvement Zone Development Authority (ANIZDA). ANIZDA oversees and manages the NIZ, a special district created by state law that is being utilized to encourage development and revitalization in center-city Allentown and along the western side of the Lehigh River.

Nelson has three sons and two grandsons, and he lives in Allentown. He enjoys sailing and traveling with his family. *Gracias, Fidel!* is his first book.

CPSIA information can be obtained
at www.ICGtesting.com
Printed in the USA
BVHW011707060423
661902BV00030B/615

9 781958 711422